Looking After Children

Guidelines

for users of the assessment and action records

London: HMSO

ISBN 0 11 321457 X

Part One

Introduction to the Records

Introduction

The assessment and action records are intended to help you if you are professionally responsible for someone else's children. They have been designed to enable you to measure children's progress, to assess the standard of care which they are receiving, and to plan improvements. You can use the records to make assessments for any child, but they are particularly relevant for monitoring the care of children who are supervised or looked after by local authorities or who are living apart from their parents in hospitals, special schools or other residential accommodation.

The forms are based on two assumptions: firstly, that local authorities and other agencies charged with the care of children separated from their families are acting *in loco parentis* and are therefore accountable for the manner in which they discharge their parental responsibilities, and secondly, that good results are dependent upon children receiving a range of experiences that will enable them to fulfil their potential. The 1989 Children Act sets as a standard of care that which 'it would be reasonable to expect a parent to give' (sect. 31). The forms use this concept as a starting point, and set out explicitly what 'reasonable parental care' might mean in practice. If you are interested in knowing more about the theoretical basis upon which the assessment and action records are constructed, we recommend reading the book which accompanies this project: *Looking After Children: Assessing Outcomes in Child Care* edited by Roy Parker, Harriet Ward, Sonia Jackson, Jane Aldgate and Peter Wedge.

Why introduce formal measures of assessment?

The 1989 Children Act emphasises the importance of planning and assessment. This is something that all parents do for their children, but which can easily be overlooked when the child is looked after away from home and responsibilities are divided among a number of different people. Of course parents would be unlikely to make the formal, written assessments that you are being asked to undertake. Nevertheless, as parents we constantly monitor our children's progress in an informal manner. We are pleased if our children do well at school, we are concerned if they appear to be unpopular, and we worry if they are frequently ill. Our feelings are related to our expectations: among other things, we want our children to be well-educated, confident, popular and healthy. As parents we also feel that we have some power to influence what happens: we try to give our children the kinds of experiences that we think will help them to achieve these aims, and if we think they are failing, we take remedial action. The assessment and action records are designed to help you, in collaboration with parents and other carers, to set out goals and make similar plans for children who are not your own, but for whom you may hold responsibility, although you may not necessarily be in daily contact with them.

You may ask why such an exercise is necessary. Do not foster carers or residential workers hold similar aims for the children under their protection and work towards their fulfilment? Does not a formal procedure such as this set children in need even further apart from their contemporaries, and reinforce the stigma of being supervised or looked after by a local authority or other corporate body? However, research has shown that careful monitoring of this kind is essential to the provision of high quality care. Children who are looked after away from home frequently move from place to place, and vital information gets lost along the way. New carers may not be aware of a child's strengths and weaknesses; they may not recognise chronic health problems; they may not know what in the past has proved to be the most successful method of dealing with a particular pattern of behaviour, and they may not know how to contact friends and other adults who are important to the child. When children are accommodated by a local authority, all those who hold parental responsibility need to know how different tasks have been allocated. Carers need to know what is important to parents, and where they disagree about suitable aims and the best methods of achieving them. Differences need to be resolved early on. Where vulnerable children are left with or returned to the care of their own parents, the quality of the experiences which they receive needs to be carefully monitored, and their progress regularly assessed.

4

The *Looking After Children* Assessment and Action Records

The records can be used to assess children's progress from birth to adulthood. They are divided into six different age-ranges: under 1, 1-2, 3-4, 5-9, 10-15 and 16 and over. The age-ranges are of varying lengths, because they have been chosen to cover different stages of development rather than specific numbers of years. In the 10-15 age-range, one or two extra questions are asked after the child reaches thirteen, but the basic structure of the form remains the same. Some sections of the form for young people aged 16 and over were designed in conjunction with the *Ready to Cope Alone* checklist. An example of this checklist, which was designed specifically for measuring young people's readiness for independent living, can be found in: Department of Health: *Patterns and Outcomes in Child Placement*, HMSO 1991.

Each form is divided into seven sections which, taken together, are intended to cover the full spectrum of development. The sections are: health, education, identity, family and social relationships, social presentation, emotional and behavioural development, and self-care skills. There is no section covering self-care skills for children under one, but otherwise you will need to look at all these developmental dimensions when assessing a child in any age-group. Although progress along these dimensions is important for all children, the particular emphasis on identity issues, relationships and behaviour reflects some of the difficulties often encountered among children who are looked after or supervised by public bodies.

Each section begins by outlining what you should be aiming at in that area with a child of a particular age, and ends by asking how far these aims are being met. As the child grows older, aims and expectations change. The education aims for a baby, for instance, are that 'the infant's physical skills are progressing normally', that 's/he is learning to communicate by smiles, gestures and elementary word sounds', that 'learning disabilities are being addressed as soon as they are recognised' and that 'the infant is active and eager to explore'. By the time the child reaches late adolescence the aims in the same dimension are that 'the young person has some educational qualifications', that 's/he is in full-time work or further education' and that 's/he has acquired special skills and interests'.

It is highly probable that children who have received low standards of care before becoming the responsibility of the local authority will perform poorly on at least some of the developmental dimensions on their first assessment. However, the records are intended not merely to measure performance, but also to identify how it might be improved. The aims which are assessed at the end of each section are closely linked to a number of practical tasks that both research and common sense suggest are necessary to their achievement. The quality of care which each child receives is assessed not only by examining how far a number of goals have been achieved, but also by asking how many of these necessary tasks have been performed for each child. For instance, at a very basic level we know that babies will not thrive unless they are given enough suitable food; therefore one question which relates to the health aim, that 'the infant is normally well and thriving in growth and development', asks about the type and quantity of food he or she receives.

These questions about necessary practical tasks are intended to break down the job of bringing up children into a series of simple steps that can be undertaken in order to improve their chances of achieving long-term well-being in adulthood. When taken, these steps combine to provide a high standard of care. We have tried to direct attention towards concrete matters, and away from more abstract considerations, not only because the former are simpler to assess, but also because it is easier for every one to understand what they are expected to do when clear-cut arrangements are made: for instance, a specific plan for the foster-carer to discuss the child's progress with the teacher and decide how he or she can be helped to produce homework on time seems more likely to produce results than a general decision to work on improving the child's school performance.

Many children in need will have encountered damaging experiences prior to your involvement. Sometimes the past will have left permanent scars no matter how good the subsequent quality of care. Nevertheless, there are many strands to children's development; the questions are intended to draw attention to those things you can do to improve their quality of life now and in the future, even though there may be other problems which cannot easily be resolved. You may find it hard when a child is, for instance, displaying multiple behaviour problems, to think about correcting his or her crooked teeth; however, severe difficulties in one area of development are not a reason for over-looking minor deficiencies in others. Also, it is well-known that success in one area tends to reverberate into others, so that, for instance, children who know that their appearance has improved are likely to have increased self-esteem, and this will give them the confidence to reach new goals in other spheres.

When all the practical tasks are accomplished, the child will be receiving the type of care that should enable him or her to meet the aims shown at the end of each section. Performance will not always improve at each assessment, for children are not passive recipients of care, and all manner of extraneous factors may intervene to frustrate the best efforts made on their behalf. Nevertheless, if you, together with the other people involved, make sure that the children for whom you are responsible receive the standard of care specified in these records, you will have given them the opportunities to reach their potential that a good parent would provide.

Part Two

How to complete the Forms

The forms have been designed to produce regular assessments of progress;they are intended for use on a six monthly, or at least an annual basis. The first completed form provides a base-line against which subsequent progress can be judged.

You may wish to use the forms in conjunction with both our basic facts sheet, which gathers information that only needs to be checked once, and our formats for making plans and conducting reviews. The complete package has been designed to meet the requirements for drawing up plans and reviewing children's cases, that are specified in the 1989 Children Act.On the other hand, the forms are extremely versatile, and can be slotted into existing reviewing and planning systems, and also used independently for assessing the quality of care received by particular groups of children. For example, when children are living with their own parents, or when care is being shared, the forms can be particularly helpful in deciding how responsibilities are to be divided; they also encourage a greater understanding of children's needs on the part of those who may not previously have realised how extensive these are. There is no reason why this method of assessment should not be used on a once-off occasion where there is particular cause for concern, although of course, there will be no means of measuring progress unless you repeat the exercise.

You will need to consult with all those people who share responsibility for the child in order to complete the form. If parents or relatives are involved with the child, then they should be included. We recommend that it should be the social worker's overall responsibility to ensure that the form is completed, although it can be filled in by the person with whom the child is living. Older children will want to play a part in the assessment themselves. To that end, the questions for young people aged 16 and over have been addressed to them directly, but they will need help in making future plans, and assessing progress. Some of the questions on the forms for younger children need to be referred to health visitors.

We do not think that it is possible to design a system which provides a comprehensive assessment of the quality of parental care and, at the same time, takes only a few minutes to complete. The Looking After Children forms are intended to set an agenda for meetings between social workers, children, parents and foster carers or residential workers, and to help everyone to think about a number of issues that are often overlooked. If you use the forms regularly, the type of questions that are asked will occur to you naturally in the course of your work, so that when the time comes for a major assessment you will already know many of the answers. Before a review it will be necessary to consult the other people involved in the child's care over any gaps that need to be filled in. Give yourself time to complete the form, and do not try to fill it in during the review or in a hurried moment just beforehand.

Some social workers worry that a formal assessment of this type will restrict conversations with clients, and make open communication more difficult. Our pilot study showed the opposite to be the case: those who took part generally found that the questions opened up new areas of discussion which had previously been difficult to introduce. If you plan to spend time discussing the issues raised and do not feel you have to move quickly on to the next question as soon as you have answered the one before, you will find that the exercise helps increase communication between all those involved.

Many teenagers will respond to the way in which you present the exercise to them: if you suggest that they are being asked to perform a dreary chore, they may well refuse to co-operate. They are much more likely to respond positively if you explain that this is an interesting way of looking at their lives so far and working out what improvements can be made.

Because the forms ask for information which is relatively time-consuming to discover we have made every effort to ensure that they are as simple as possible to complete. Thus, open-ended questions have largely been avoided, and almost all replies take the form of multiple choice answers that can be indicated with a tick in an appropriate box.

The questions at the end of each section that ask how far specific goals have been achieved, are usually answered by marking the child's position on a linear scale. A mark towards the left-hand end of the scale suggests that the child is performing poorly on this particular indicator and a mark towards the right-hand end suggests that he or she is performing well. These scaled questions should, as far as possible, be completed by the same person each time the child's progress is assessed, in order to ensure that judgments are as consistent as possible. We recommend that social workers answer these questions on the form for young people of 16 and over.

All the questions follow a similar format. For instance, one of the health questions for children in most age ranges asks whether the child has seen a dentist since the last review, and if all dental recommendations have been carried out. If the answer is yes, tick the appropriate boxes, and then move on to the next question; if, however, any of the answers are 'no' or 'don't know', then you are asked to decide who will take further action. You may need to complete more than one box for this: for instance, the parent may need to find out whether any treatment is outstanding, while the foster carer may need to arrange and accompany the child to his or her next appointment. In this case, the plan will be fairly simple, and you are only asked to indicate who will be responsible for carrying it out. Where the issues are more complex, you are also asked to specify what you have decided to do. In some instances, there may be a good reason for a decision not to proceed further. The child in question may, for instance, be settling in with new foster carers and be apprehensive about leaving the house; you may decide that perhaps his or her dental care can safely be left for a short period. Records may have been lost, and you may not be able to find out whether the child has ever visited a dentist before. The final box is for you to provide an explanation for negative replies.

Make sure that you always complete the 'explanation' box. Sometimes you may want to take a particular action, but insufficient resources or other constraints will prevent you from doing so. If that is the case then say so. Otherwise those who monitor the overall provision made for children in your department will not know about the difficulties encountered at grass-roots level.

You should answer *all* the questions on the form. Where there is any disagreement about a reply, this should be written on the record.

Summaries

Each form ends with a summary of the work that needs to be undertaken to improve the quality of care the child receives. Complete this
as you go along, and record the plans made, the person to whom the
work has been delegated, and the target dates that have been agreed
for its completion. This summary of ongoing work should be checked
whenever a statutory review is held and, in fact, is duplicated in the
review form that can be used as part of our package.

Measuring change: a note to reviewing officers, managers and researchers

The replies to the questions on the forms will identify areas where children's progress is slow or standards of care are poor. A second assessment will demonstrate how the situation has changed in the interven-
ing months. We suggest, however, that those who wish to make more
precise assessments look more closely at the replies to the *aims* questions, the *summaries*, the *explanations* that are given for negative
replies, and the *factual information* that is recorded on our basic facts
sheets or on the file.

The answers to the 'aims' questions at the end of each section will indicate how much progress a child is making in the seven key areas of
development. Most of these questions are answered by marking a
child's position on a linear scale. These scales are all 5 centimetres
long. Answers can be coded using a transparent ruler and giving the
reply a value from one to five, depending on the centimetre in which
the mark falls. Replies to subsequent assessments can be similarly
coded, and the results compared. Linear scales are also used for many
of the answers to the questions concerning a child's emotional and
behavioural development; replies can be evaluated in exactly the same
way.

If the replies to the 'aims' questions show that a child, or a group of
children, appears to be progressing slowly on any particular dimension, the answers to the preceding questions in that section should be
scrutinized. These should show you what improvements could be
made to the standard of care. Decisions to undertake specific tasks are
recorded on the summaries. These should also spell out who has taken

responsibility for the work, what are the target dates for action, and whether these have been met. Sometimes there will be a decision not to undertake a particular piece of work. The reason for this should be recorded in the 'explanation' box. These explanations should give information not only about casework decisions, but also about inadequate resources, bureaucratic restrictions, and constraints on social workers' time.

Factual information that does not need to be repeatedly checked is not recorded on the assessment and action records. A number of questions do, however, direct those who make the assessments to gather such information, and record it elsewhere. We recommend that this information, which covers such matters as immunisations, examination results and changes of placement, is recorded on the basic facts sheets that have been designed as part of this project. File notes and facesheets can also be used for this purpose. Using the Looking After Children system of assessment should ensure that valuable factual information is also available for analysis.

Part Three

Points about specific questions

HEALTH

All children:

Statutory medicals:

There is a legal requirement that each child looked after by a local authority should receive a medical examination before placement if at all possible, otherwise as soon as possible afterwards.

From then onwards, statutory medical examinations must be given at least once every six months before the child's second birthday, and at least once a year afterwards.

Young people of 16 and over have a right to withhold their consent to medical examination and treatment; children under 16 may also refuse their consent if *the doctor* decides that they are of sufficient understanding to appreciate the consequences of refusal.

Recommended developmental reviews:

District health authorities have their own schemes of health and developmental surveillance which are usually undertaken jointly by general practitioners and health visitors. Young children are usually reviewed at:

6–8 weeks
6–9 months
18–24 months
36–42 months

You may find that if the child has statutory medical examinations, these will include regular developmental surveillance, but you should check that this is the case. It is important not to overlook developmental reviews, as these are where health problems such as dislocated hips, sight and hearing impairment and learning difficulties are often first noticed. Such conditions often require prompt and early treatment.

Measuring the child's height and weight:

It is extremely important to keep a close watch on the growth rates of vulnerable children. Children tend to grow at a regular rate along a recognised curve (centile). They may stop thriving when emotionally upset, when ill, or when inadequately fed. They may also put on too much weight when unhappy or when given an unsuitable diet, and this will affect their self-esteem and health in adulthood. One cannot judge growth on a single measurement, but an unexpected change in growth *rate* should be viewed with concern. It is therefore important to measure a child's height and weight at regular intervals, and to check that he or she is growing at a normal rate. To do this, you will need to know the centiles along which the child is growing; this can be done easily by using the charts that appear on the following pages. The charts can also be used to translate inches into centimetres, and pounds into kilograms. Children who cross two or more centiles should be referred for evaluation. Centile charts of vulnerable pre-school children should be kept by health visitors and general practitioners; those of older children should be kept by school nurses. You should make certain that growth charts of vulnerable children *are* being kept and updated; if not, it is advisable to keep a chart on the file, and plot height and weight yourself.

Centile Charts

These are shown, for ease of reference, on the following two pairs of facing pages (16 and 17, 18 and 19).

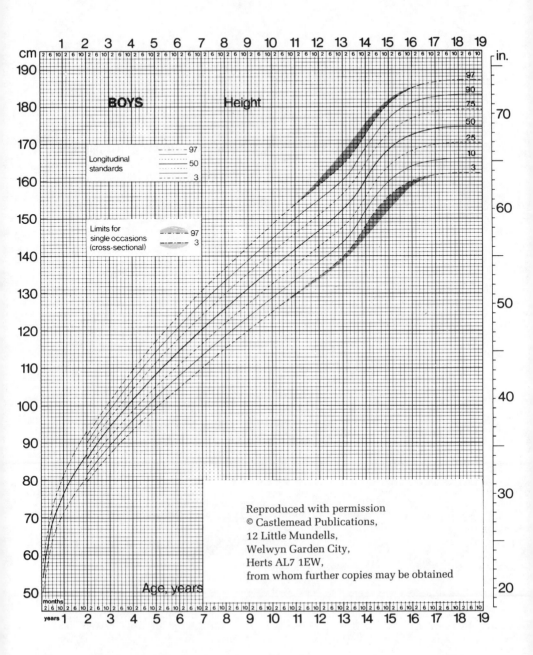

BOYS Height

Longitudinal standards — 97, 50, 3

Limits for single occasions (cross-sectional) 97, 3

Age, years

Reproduced with permission
© Castlemead Publications,
12 Little Mundells,
Welwyn Garden City,
Herts AL7 1EW,
from whom further copies may be obtained

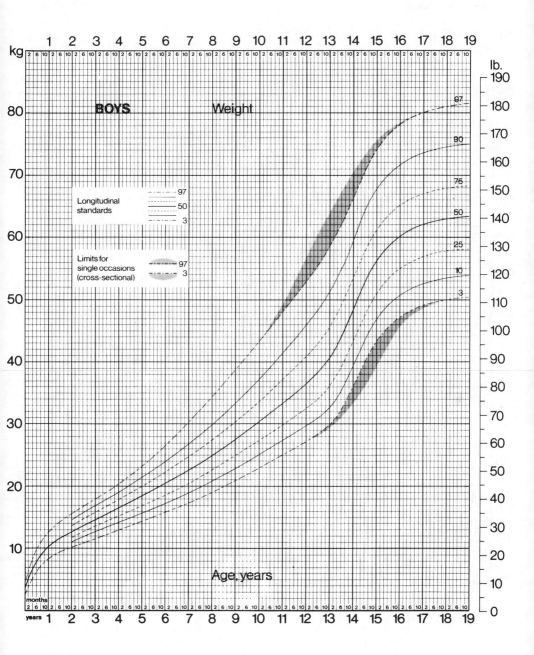

BOYS Weight

Longitudinal standards
97
50
3

Limits for single occasions (cross-sectional)
97
3

Age, years

kg

lb.

months

years

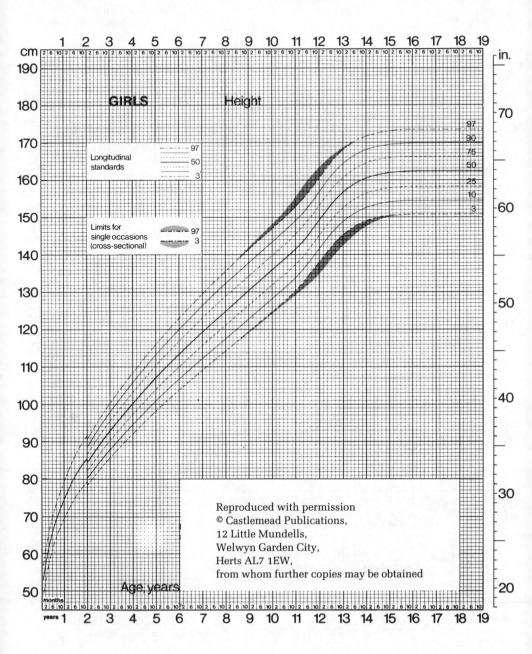

GIRLS Height

Longitudinal standards
— · — · 97
———— 50
·········· 3

Limits for single occasions (cross-sectional)
97
3

Reproduced with permission
© Castlemead Publications,
12 Little Mundells,
Welwyn Garden City,
Herts AL7 1EW,
from whom further copies may be obtained

Age, years

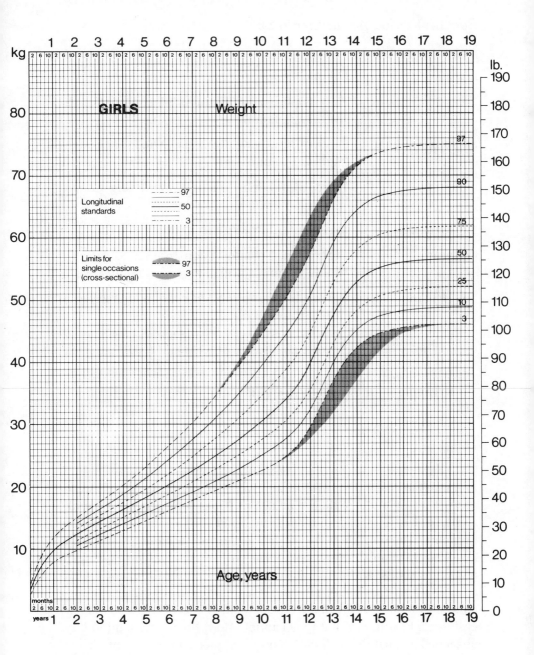

GIRLS Weight

Longitudinal standards
— · — 97
········· 50
— · · — 3

Limits for single occasions (cross-sectional)
97
3

kg

Age, years

Recommended immunisations:

These are as follows:

Age due:	Immunisation:
2 months	First Diphtheria, Tetanus, Whooping Cough (Pertussis), Polio
3 months	Second Diphtheria, Tetanus, Whooping Cough (Pertussis), Polio
4 months	Third Diphtheria, Tetanus, Whooping Cough (Pertussis), Polio
12–18 months	Measles, Mumps, Rubella (MMR)
4–5 years	Diphtheria, Tetanus, Polio (pre-school boost), Measles, Mumps, Rubella (*if not already given*)
10–14 years	Rubella (*girls only if MMR not already received*) Heaf test and BCG (*in some districts BCG is given selectively to high-risk babies at birth and it will not need repeating*)
15–18 years	Tetanus and Polio

Diet:

The connection between diet and health is now well-recognised. It is important to check that children and babies under three not only have enough to eat, but that their diet also includes sufficient solids, milk and vitamins. The health visitor is the most suitable person to advise over this. The checklists for foods for children aged three and over should help you discover whether the child has a sufficient quantity of healthy foods, and does not over-indulge in unhealthy foods such as sweets and fizzy drinks. Recent research has shown that poor parents are generally aware of the type of foods that are beneficial to their children's health, but that they cannot afford them, and tend to buy cheaper, less heathly foods which have a higher calorie content. Points such as these should be discussed with the carers, and, if necessary, indicated in the 'explanations' box.

Dental care:

Dental care should begin as soon as the teeth appear. Children who have had a very poor diet sometimes have teeth which are already decayed when they come through, and should be taken to a dentist immediately this becomes apparent. All children should be taken regularly to a dentist from two years of age. The dentist will give advice on whether fluoride supplements are necessary.

Infants aged 0–1 years, 1–2 years

Milestones:

Babies develop according to a recognised pattern. 'Milestones' are the ages at which the child first smiles, sits, crawls, walks and so on. These should be monitored, as notably slow development can be indicative of other problems. For most milestones the range of normality is very wide; the health visitor is the most suitable person to advise over this.

Children aged 10–15 years, 16 and over

Advice and information about contraception and sexually transmitted diseases:

Our pilot study found that a surprisingly large number of teenagers had been given little or no advice on this subject. It cannot be assumed that all children will receive adequate sexual education in school, for vulnerable children often truant, or change schools and miss the relevant lessons. Sexually active girls should be aware that contraceptive pills give them no protection against AIDS; and teenagers of both sexes should be advised of the protection afforded by condoms. Someone should talk over these and similar issues with the teenager concerned: it is not enough to hand out written information which may be misunderstood, or left unread.

EDUCATION

Infants and children aged under 1, 1–2, 3–4 years

Education begins at birth. Through exploring their environment, experimenting with a variety of stimulating toys and other playthings and interacting with adults and other children, babies and toddlers learn early educational skills. This preparation is just as important as the formal education they will later receive, and the questions in this section should be answered with as much care for younger children as for those who have started school.

Children aged 5–9, 10–15 years

Learning special skills, clubs, sports, school outings and residential trips:

Many vulnerable children miss out on extra-curricular activities because they involve additional expense. Foster carers can be deterred from claiming additional expenses if the procedure is too complicated. Yet it is through activities such as these that children become confident of their own abilities, and learn to socialise with others. Your replies to the questions on these forms can provide valuable information about the extent of need in your area; if carers cannot afford to provide children with these types of experience, please indicate this in the 'explanations' box.

Unscheduled changes of school:

These are not planned transitions from first to middle school or from junior to secondary schools, but unplanned changes that cause additional disruption in the lives of already vulnerable children. Parents will often make strenuous efforts to ensure continuity in their children's education and will put off moving house or changing jobs while their children are preparing for GCSEs, for instance. Similar efforts should be made for children looked after away from home, and changes of school should be regarded as serious events, that need not automatically accompany changes of placement.

Children aged 10–15 years:

GCSE subjects:

These are usually discussed and agreed with teachers in the spring term of school year nine (i.e. at age 13 plus). This is a very important point in a child's educational career and it is essential that the full implications of the choices made are understood and discussed. The child may need support to do subjects that fit in with his or her individual interests and future plans rather than the school's convenience.

National Insurance

National Insurance cards are automatically issued to young people in receipt of child benefit when they reach 15 years 6 months. Young people who are looked after by local authorities may not receive child benefit and therefore will need to make a separate application to be registered for National Insurance.

IDENTITY

Children from ethnic minority groups:

Children who are looked after away from home often find it difficult to develop a clear sense of identity. Those who come from ethnic minority groups and who are placed with families of dissimilar cultural backgrounds may find their situation particularly confusing. There is at present some controversy as to whether, when no matching foster home can be found, it is better to place children with foster carers from a different ethnic group, rather than leave them in residential homes, where there may still be no one who shares their culture. Whatever decision is made about placement, it is important to make sure that the carers are aware of the particular needs of ethnic minority children: children who come from ethnic minority groups may be accustomed to a special diet, their first language may not be English, they may follow a different religion. The customs and culture of different ethnic minority groups bear little similarity to one another. Many of the questions in this section are designed to ensure that ethnic minority children retain links with their original culture and are taught acceptable ways of dealing with the discrimination that all too many will experience.

Infants and children aged under 1, 1–2, 3–4, 5–9 years

Teaching the child his or her name:

Names are also symbols that are crucially tied up with a child's sense of identity. It is important for foster carers to learn how to pronounce the names of children and parents correctly. Children whose family structures have changed may be known by more than one surname: it is helpful to children if a definite decision can be made about what they are to be called before they start school.

Infants and children aged under 1, 1–2, 3–4, 5–9 years

Life story books:

Start collecting photographs and noting down addresses when children are very small, even if they are not yet old enough to talk about their early life. Knowing where they used to live, who looked after them and what they and their former carers used to look like helps children develop a sense of identity; this is particularly valuable because if there is a change of placement or social worker, those who take over responsibility for the child may find it impossible to gather lost information.

Young people aged 16 and over

Dealing with discrimination:

Not all young people will be *victims* of discrimination: some will deal with it by joining in. This question is intended to be applicable to both the perpetrators and the victims of racism and other forms of prejudice. Do not only ask whether young people who have been victimised have learnt how to cope; also consider if the perpetrators need further advice in confronting their prejudices.

FAMILY AND SOCIAL RELATIONSHIPS

Children aged 10–15 years

Opportunities to belong to a church or other religious body:

This question has been included not only because it is important to consider children's spiritual needs, but also because membership of a religious organisation can give vulnerable children the emotional support and acceptance that they so often need. If neither child nor carers have any interest in religion, this should be indicated in the 'explanation' box.

SOCIAL PRESENTATION

All children

When you are deciding whether a child appears well cared for, remember that white carers may need to learn how to look after black children's hair and skin. Black children's skin becomes dry and flaky unless it is given proper attention.

EMOTIONAL AND BEHAVIOURAL DEVELOPMENT

All children

Answering the questions:

Many of the questions in this section are answered by marking the child's position on a linear scale. Do this in the same way as you have answered the 'aims' questions at the end of each section. The results will be most consistent if the same person always fills in these answers. The carer, who has most first-hand experience of any behaviour problems, may be the best person to answer these questions. A child's behaviour can be the main reason why he or she is looked after away from home. Changes in behaviour must therefore be carefully monitored; movements along the linear scale should show how behaviour has altered during the period between assessments.

Treatment of behaviour problems:

If a child does display any emotional or behavioural problems you are asked to describe how they are being dealt with. Make sure that this section is filled in: discipline is an issue which needs to be discussed, and over which there may well be disagreements. It is important that all those who share in the care of a child have an opportunity to discuss their methods of dealing with difficult behaviour so that there can be some consistency in the treatment the child receives.

Make sure that foster carers are aware that they are not expected to cope with difficult behaviour unaided. Arranging for a child to be referred to the school psychological service or to a child guidance clinic should be regarded as a means of providing additional assistance, and not as an admission of failure.

Experience of abuse:

Remember that children can be perpetrators as well as victims of abuse, and that those who have experienced damaging relationships with adults may respond by abusing their brothers and sisters or schoolmates. This question is intended to be applicable both to perpetrators and victims. Specify what the problem is when you explain what additional help and/or protection the child needs.

Children aged 10–15 years

Statements:

Statements of special educational needs were introduced in the Education Act 1981. They were intended to be used as a means of directing extra resources towards children with special needs, but they are often used to exclude older children with behaviour problems from a particular school. Children whose behaviour is difficult to contain may be suspended pending a statement of special needs, and then be obliged to wait several more months for transfer to another school. In this way they may be excluded from school for months on end. For children who have no identifiable physical or mental handicap, statementing must be regarded as a negative measure of educational outcome.

SELF-CARE SKILLS

All children
Different children acquire these skills at very different rates. Our pilot study found that some children regarded the checklist as quite chal-

lenging, while others found it was very easy. If you have used the Looking After Children scheme to assess this child before, refer back to the earlier assessment of self-care skills, and ask only about those which the child had not acquired on the previous occasion. Although most of these skills will not be forgotten once they have been acquired, remember that children whose lives have been recently disrupted may regress, and a more thorough assessment may be necessary in these circumstances.

CONCLUSION

The Looking After Children scheme is not intended as a bureaucratic exercise, but as a means of helping you and the other people involved to work out what can be done to influence outcomes for children who may be seriously disadvantaged. Your replies will provide the information that is necessary to plan improvements; above all, the exercise should help you perform an extremely difficult job more effectively, and we hope that all those who participate will find it both useful and enjoyable.

Printed in the United Kingdom by HMSO
Dd 295221 C15 11/91 Ed(293305)